IF I WERE A LIGHTHOUSE

Written by
Richard Rensberry

Illustrated by Mary Rensberry

Copyright © 2017, Richard Rensberry

All rights reserved.

No part of this publication may be reproduced, stored in a retrieval system or transmitted in any form or by any means electronic, mechanical, photo-copied, recorded or otherwise, without the prior written permission of the publisher and authors.

Published by: QuickTurtle Books LLC®

http://www.richardrensberry.com

ISBN: 978-1-940736-36-5
Published in the United States of America

This book is dedicated to the current and future preservation of Crisp Point Lighthouse. May our children and their children know and appreciate its vital presence like the multitude of ships that navigated across the history of Lake Superior. May Crisp Point Lighthouse forever stand noble as a brilliant beacon to us all.

        Richard and Mary Rensberry
             Paradise, Michigan
              August 4, 2018

If I were a lighthouse,
I'd shine glowing bright

like a smile on the lips
of a coal-black night.

If I were a lighthouse,
I'd have chores to do—
guide the ship's captain
with its gallant crew.

If I were a lighthouse,
their vessels would crawl
safe within my harbor
through fog and squall.

If I were a lighthouse,
seagulls would soar
over windswept rocks
on my Great Lakes shore.

If I were a lighthouse,
I'd weather out the mists
huddled against the storms
that hammer my cliffs.

If I were a lighthouse,
I'd wink my bright eye
beneath the North Star
in the night-time sky.

If I were a lighthouse,
I'd always stand avail
so great ships could pass
with their flags of regale.

If I were a lighthouse
I'd shine glowing bright
like a smile on the lips
of a coal-black night.

The End

Please visit QuickTurtle Books® on Amazon
and kindly leave a review.

Much appreciated!

More QuickTurtle Books® in the Rhyme for Young Readers Series

Big Ships
The Siren of Mackinaw
I Wish It Were Christmas
Goblin's Goop
Monster Monster
How the Snake Got It's Tail
If I Were A Garden
If I Were A Caterpillar
Colors Talk
Abigail's Chickens
If I Were A Heart
If I Were A Blossom
Trick or Treat
Grandma's Quilt
If I Were A Book
The Blind Dove
The Burrow Babbit
I Wish I Could

Rhyme for Young Readers Glossary

1. gallant- brave

2. squall- a sudden gust of wind with rain or snow.

3. Great Lakes- the big lakes surrounding the State of Michigan.

4. avail- of use to.

5. regale- delight with something pleasing.

Made in the USA
San Bernardino, CA
11 April 2019